21 THINGS

Worth Knowing About

By

Peter McIntosh

ISBN 979-8-89686-551-3

Contents

Introduction

Congratulations on purchasing this book!

Within these pages, you'll discover 21 thought-provoking topics, each offering a concise yet impactful perspective. The book explores everyday challenges and provides thoughtful proposals for navigating them effectively.

What sets this book apart is its poetic format—succinct and powerful, allowing you to connect with the advice on a deeper, more emotional level than traditional chapters might provide.

Each poem stems from personal experiences, reflecting lessons I've learned and strategies I've found most effective. Through these verses, I aim to share practical insights that can inspire and guide you in tackling life's daily challenges.

I hope the subtle guidance and reflections offered here will help you cultivate a balanced and thoughtful approach to life. These lessons have been invaluable in shaping my perspective, and I trust they can do the same for you.

Take a moment to reflect on the advice in each poem. Consider how it applies to your life and embark on a journey of self-discovery and growth. Start today—evaluate these learnings and see how they can transform your outlook and experiences.

Moving Forward

The Power of Small Steps

With every step, though small or great,
We rise to meet the hands of fate.
In tasks that seem so dull and bland,
We give our best, with steady hand.

For in the mundane, there's a spark,
A chance to leave a lasting mark.
Each little deed, each thoughtful act,
Adds value, kindness, that's a fact.

No task too small, no goal too high,
With every effort, we reach the sky.
A positive heart, a forward view,
Moves mountains, makes the old seem new.

So press ahead with all your might,

Even when the road seems tight.

For in each moment, do your best,

And you'll find peace and endless rest.

Handling Conflict

The Quiet Path

When tempers flare and voices rise,

It's easy to believe the world's unwise.

But in the heat of each dispute,

The deeper truth may not compute.

For all are fighting battles, unseen,

In hearts and minds, where wounds have been.

Their anger may not be meant for you,

But for struggles that they've yet to undo.

So, when the storm begins to brew,

Remember, they may need kindness too.

With calmness, choose to step aside,

And see the pain they try to hide.

No need for anger, no need for fight,

Just open eyes and hearts alight.

For when we see the truth within,

We heal the world where we begin.

Being Prepared

The Power of Preparation

I once joined a hackathon with zeal,
Full of ideas, but unsure what's real.
My mind raced fast, but I had to learn,
Preparation's the key to help things turn.

I fumbled through tasks, a lesson so clear,
Without a plan, things quickly disappear.
The code that I wrote didn't quite align,
A failure in focus, no clear design.

Then came a meeting, with a customer to meet,
I thought I knew it all but faced defeat.
Unprepared, I stumbled, lost in the flow,
And the embarrassment hit me—hard, a blow.

That moment, it struck, deep down in my soul,

The truth about preparation, the key to control.

It's not just about showing up with might,

But the thought and the effort, to get it right.

Now I plan, I study, I make my way clear,

For in preparation, I have no fear.

From hackathons to meetings,

the lesson's the same,

To be prepared is to win the game.

Learning From Your Mistakes

The Gift of Mistakes

I've stumbled and fallen, tripped on the way,

Made choices I regret, more than I can say.

But with every misstep, every fall and bruise,

I've learned a little more about what to choose.

Mistakes are teachers, not foes to fight,

They show me my flaws, but also my might.

For through the cracks

and the moments of doubt,

I've found the strength to turn things about.

Each error, a lesson, wrapped in disguise,

A chance to grow, to open my eyes.

I've learned from the hurt,

the wrongs and the tears,

To face what's ahead, without fear or fears.

So now I embrace what once made me weak,

For the wisdom gained is what I now seek.

I stand tall and stronger, no longer in haste,

For the greatest gift is learning from mistakes.

Getting Along with Others

The Dance of Understanding

In a world that spins with voices loud,

It's not about the crowd you're in,

But the way you listen, calm and proud,

And how you let the silence win.

You don't have to be likeable, just kind,

A genuine interest, a heart that's wide,

Don't criticise, condemn, or bind

With judgments that we often hide.

Remember names, they're keys to hearts,

And in the listening, real trust starts.

Encourage others to share their say,

With patience, hear them every day.

Begin in friendship, warm and true,

Understand their point of view,

What makes them tick, what makes them feel,

A bond is built with words that heal.

Be helpful, humble, lend a hand,

And know the strength of where you stand.

For you are who you are because,

Of partnerships and their sweet cause.

What if the other's right today?

Is there a third way, a kinder way?

For listening speaks a thousand times,

More than any judgment or climb.

If you don't hear, you say they're gone,

Their voice unheard, their being drawn.

Respect and patience, let it flow,

And through this grace, you both will grow.

So let it go, let go of strife,

In understanding, you'll find life.

For getting along is more than chance,

It's the beauty of a gentle dance.

Comparing Yourself to Others

The Path of Your Own

Don't compare yourself to others' ways,

Each one walks their path,

through nights and days.

In the game of life, in every role,

It's not about the score, but the heart and soul.

Like golf, "play the course," it's yours to tread,

With every swing, each step ahead.

The course may twist, the fairways long,

But it's your rhythm, your pace, your song.

The world will call and voices may rise,

But when you look within, you see no disguise.

Who judges you when you stand alone?

The mirror reflects what you have grown.

There's no need to measure, no need to race,

In your own time, find your own grace.

Each step you take, each choice you make,

Builds who you are, no need to fake.

So trust the journey, let others be,

For in the end, it's only you, you need to see.

Work to improve, but never compare,

You're a unique story, beyond compare.

The Importance of Good Daily Habits

The Power of Small Habits

Good habits build, like brick by brick,
Each day a step, each choice you pick.
It's in the little things, so pure and small,
That shape your life, that make you whole.

Bad habits, too, yield their own result,
Five years passed by, no plan to consult.
A life that drifts with no health in mind,
A future that lags, with time left behind.

You don't get fit with one giant leap,
It's not a sprint, but a steady sweep.
A twelve-hour session won't change the tide,
It's daily effort, with patience as your guide.

A walk, a stretch, a mindful pause,

The smallest acts create the cause.

For fitness grows, not in haste,

But in the rhythm of a steady pace.

So cultivate habits, good and true,

Little by little, they will renew.

Your health, your mind, your body's grace,

Built by the steps you daily embrace.

Each choice you make, each thing you do,

Is a seed for the future, a garden to strew.

Start small today, don't wait for the grand,

For little habits lead to where you stand.

Motivating Others

The Art of Lifting Others

To motivate, to lift, to cheer,

Is to see the good, to hold it near.

Give honest praise, sincere, true,

A word of kindness goes far through.

Praise the good with open heart,

Allow them space to play their part.

When feedback's tough, let grace be shown,

Let people grow, let them be known.

Sometimes an idea, they'll think it's theirs,

But guide them gently, show you care.

Let them lead, let them take flight,

In their success, share the light.

Be helpful, be kind in all you do,

Lend a hand, stay honest too.

Optimism fuels the soul, the mind,

It sparks the strength that we can find.

Do what's right, not what's easy,

For good will come, though roads be breezy.

Try your best and let it be,

Worry not about the rest, just see.

For in the end, we rise as one,

When we help each other, we've all won.

So lift them up, with hope, with care,

For when we're kind, we're always there.

Accepting other People's Ideas
for You

The Gifts That Others Bring

Sometimes, the perfect thing comes near,
Not by our hand, but someone dear.
A choice they make, a thought they share,
That fits us perfectly, beyond compare.

We don't always know what's best for us,
And that's okay, in this world so vast.
Sometimes it works to let them choose,
To trust their hearts, their love infused.

Accept the happy coincidences that flow,
Like a situation that appeared, aglow.
A gift, a surprise, with no plan at all,
A blessing that arrived with no call.

Life's little gifts can come unbidden,

In the kindness of others, our hearts are ridden.

We learn from their wisdom, their point of view,

Their ideas, their actions, so bright and true.

So when the perfect thing is placed in sight,

Don't hesitate, let it feel right.

For sometimes the best is found in chance,

In the hands of others, in their dance.

Partnerships

The Strength of Partnership

A partnership is built on care,

A bond that's strong, beyond compare.

Respect, the foundation, steady and true,

Where each feels valued,

seen through and through.

Do not undermine, or tear apart,

But lift them up, and guard their heart.

In unity, there's strength to grow,

Together, we rise, together we flow.

Let go of friction, let it fade,

For peace in partnership is lovingly made.

In selfless service, we plant the seed,

So others may find the shade they need.

It's not about the glory, the fame,

But about the good that we can claim.

The joy in giving, the warmth in grace,

Building a world that we embrace.

So let your partnership shine with care,

With respect, with love, with hearts that share.

In every step, in every way,

Together we flourish, come what may.

Managing Stress

Finding Calm Amidst the Storm

The past is gone, it's done and through,

No need to dwell on what you can't undo.

Learn from it, let it guide your way,

But leave it behind, don't let it sway.

Plan for the future, set your sights high,

But don't let worry cloud the sky.

Focus on now, the habits you keep,

In the present moment, find peace so deep.

Be grateful for all that you've received,

For the small things, for the joy you've believed.

In every breath, in every stride,

Gratitude opens the door inside.

Breathe deeply, with rhythm and grace,

The Wimhof method, in its embrace.

Inhale the calm, exhale the stress,

In each breath, find stillness, no less.

Manage your stress, one breath at a time,

With patience, with purpose,

your peace will climb.

The past is behind, the future's unknown,

But in the present, you are never alone.

Procrastination

The Trap of Procrastination

A task awaits, but you hesitate,

The moment's here, yet you procrastinate.

Thoughts swirl, but action stays behind,

The clock ticks on, yet peace you can't find.

You say, "Tomorrow, I'll begin,"

But tomorrow never comes, it's always dim.

The longer you wait, the harder it seems,

The mountain grows, from simple dreams.

But there's a trick, a way to win,

5-4-3-2-1, and then begin.

Don't think, don't wait, just start the race,

In that first step, find your grace.

Do it now, and it's done,

Procrastination loses, and you've won.

The task is simple once you start,

For action flows from an open heart.

So break the chains, let them fall,

And in that first move, you'll stand tall.

The hardest part is starting, it's true,

But once you begin, there's nothing to undo.

Dealing with change

The Seed and the Storm

Amid the winds, so wild and vast,
Where shadows fall and doubts hold fast,
A tiny seed begins to grow,
Its roots dig deep, though tempests blow.

The storm may howl, the skies may weep,
Yet through the dark, it will not sleep.
Its strength, unseen, it draws from earth,
Each trial a testament to rebirth.

For every gale that bends the tree
Unveils a hidden strength set free.
The cracks in stone let light shine through,
Each wound, a chance to start anew.

So rise, dear soul, embrace the fight,

For even night births morning's light.

Each stumble marks a lesson learned,

Each loss, a bridge to what's yet earned.

Opportunities, like fleeting streams,

Flow swiftly past in whispered dreams.

But seize them bold, with steady hand,

And shape your fate from shifting sand.

For resilience is the root of might,

A beacon blazing through the night.

And every chance, a door ajar—

A step to reach your brightest star!

Goals

The Journey to Clarity

The hardest part is knowing the way,

Not the task ahead or the price we pay.

It's in the choice, the dreams we hold,

To define our life, to be bold.

What do you want your life to be?

A path of purpose, wild and free.

But how to choose, how to see,

The steps that lead to what you'll be?

Listen to others, their voices, their dreams,

Their ideas may spark your own gleams.

Yet in the end, it's your truth to find,

What you want, what fills your mind.

Figure it out, carve it clear,

What does your life truly hold dear?

Then say no to what pulls you astray,

To what distracts you, or leads you away.

For life's too short to wander lost,

To chase every path at any cost.

Stand firm, say no, let your vision grow,

And walk the path where your true self glows.

Experiment and Explore

The Leap of Trust

Trust is a leap, a daring flight,

A willingness to step into the night.

To experiment, to explore,

To seek the unknown, to ask for more.

It's a risk, a chance to grow,

To let go of the past, to let life flow.

The fear of falling may hold us tight,

But trust whispers softly, "Take the flight."

For in each step, in every fall,

We know we'll be caught, we'll stand tall.

The safety net is not just seen,

But felt within, unseen, serene.

With confidence, we chase our dreams,

Trusting the journey, trusting the seams.

The world may wobble, the road may bend,

But we're looked after, from start to end.

So take the risk, explore, be bold,

Let trust unfold its story told.

For when we leap with faith in hand,

We find the strength to understand.

Commitment

All In

The nice thing about life, you see,

Is that you're "all in," no matter where you be.

Each moment counts, each breath a play,

We're bound to the game, come what may.

No matter what you choose to do,

You're part of the ride, it's all up to you.

So why not make it a game that's grand,

With every step, take a bold stand.

While you wait, while time moves fast,

Why not make this moment last?

Pick the best thing, the one that sings,

The path that joy and meaning brings.

Do you have anything better to do?

Than to live a life that's rich and true?

Why not take the chance, why not dream big,

Play the game with passion, dance the jig.

For life's a gift, you're all in,

So choose the best, let the adventure begin.

Play magnificently, with heart and soul,

And watch your life become your goal.

Letting Go

In this moment

The actions, thoughts, the words they say,

Are not yours to hold or guide today.

The opinions of others, like passing breeze,

Are theirs to carry, not yours to please.

You cannot control what they may think,

Their judgments, their whispers, on the brink.

Like leaves that fall and drift away,

Their thoughts will shift, come what may.

The past is gone, it cannot be changed,

A chapter closed, no matter how estranged.

The future's unknown, a path unclear,

No need to fret, no need to fear.

For what you control is in your heart,

The present moment, where you start.

In each thought you choose,

in each step you take,

Find peace in knowing you can make or break.

Let go of others' views and sway,

And live your truth in your own way.

For the past and future aren't yours to steer,

But now, in this moment, you hold dear.

Challenging Yourself

Strength Under Load

You'll never know just what you can do,

If you never face a challenge, see it through.

For strength is born not in ease or light,

But in the struggle, in the fight.

When burdened with weight,

when pushed to the edge,

You'll find new power, make a pledge.

For it's under load that muscles grow,

And deeper roots in the soil you sow.

The pressure reveals the strength inside,

The limits stretch with each new stride.

It's when you carry, when you strive,

That you uncover the will to thrive.

So don't shy away from the weight you bear,

For it's in the load that you learn to dare.

Only then, with heart so bold,

Will you see the power you truly hold.

The Foundation of Trust

Trust

Trust is a blend, a sacred art,
A dance of mind, of soul, of heart.
It's built on three, entwined and true,
Each one essential to see you through.

First, be authentic, true to who you are,
No masks to wear, no false façade,
For trust begins when you are real,
When others know the truth you feel.

Then comes logic, solid and clear,
Decisions made without fear.
Thoughts grounded in reason, firm and sound,
A steady course where truth is found.

And third, directed empathy, a guiding hand,

To understand, to truly stand.

In another's shoes, with care you see,

Their feelings, their thoughts, their deepest plea.

But if one wavers, if one's not strong,

Trust begins to falter, to go wrong.

For trust requires these threads entwined,

In perfect balance, heart and mind.

So be authentic, think with care,

Empathize, with love to share.

And in this balance, trust will stay,

Guiding you both, day by day.

Understanding Others

Reactions

To understand why people act the way they do,
Imagine a fire alarm, blaring loud and true.
Each person's response, unique and clear,
Reveals their nature, their deepest fear.

Some may deny, calm as can be,
"Only a test," they say, "no need to flee."
They question not, they stand in place,
Trusting the sound, not the urgent race.

Others may panic, hearts filled with doubt,
"There must be a fire," they rush to get out.
Fear takes the lead, and urgency's clear,
They act swiftly, driven by fear.

And some will pause, with thoughtful mind,

Questioning if the fire's real, or merely designed.

They'll move with care, no rush or haste,

A middle ground, not a frantic pace.

By watching their reactions, you see what's true,

How they process fear, what they value,

Whether they act on instinct,

or take time to assess,

Shows how they handle chaos, and handle stress.

So next time you wonder, when people react,

Think of the fire alarm, and trace the track.

Some rush, some wait, some calmly decide,

Each response a window to the heart inside.

Love

Love

Romantic love, a burst of light,
A spark that catches, burning bright.
It's energy, an electric charge,
A pull that makes the heart enlarge.

In gazes held, in touches sweet,
In physical beauty, hearts compete.
A dance of chemistry, fiery and pure,
Attraction draws us to allure.

Reason steps in, soft and true,
A bond that forms in me and you.
An agreement made, a shared design,
To be an "item," hearts combine.

But love, true love, is far more deep,

It's not the rush, nor feelings steep.

It's energy, but steady, sure,

A calm connection that will endure.

Reason, too, plays its part,

In love that grows from open heart.

It's not the thrill of fleeting fire,

But a foundation built with care and desire.

Love is patient, love is kind,

It's in the quiet, the peace we find.

It doesn't need the flash or show,

For love endures, and gently grows.

Romantic love may burn so bright,

But love is steady, a constant light.

A blend of reason, trust, and grace,

Love is the bond that time can't erase.

Epilogue/Conclusion

I hope you've found this book
both useful and enjoyable.

In the future, I plan to create a traditional chapter
book that will delve deeper into the specific
experiences that shaped the insights and
conclusions shared in these poems.

This upcoming work will offer a more detailed
exploration, providing greater context and a
richer understanding of the lessons conveyed
here.